# Raspberry Pi

*(101 Beginners Guide)*

*The Definitive Step by Step guide for what you need to know to get started*

# Table of Contents

# Introduction to Raspberry Pi

Are you a person who loves to be in the know when it comes to the latest technological advances and breakthroughs? Perhaps you are a teacher who would like to teach your students about computer science and information technology, but you cannot attain the resources to do so. Even if you are the parent of a child who loves to learn new things, explore and create, the Raspberry Pi is the product for you.

This microcomputer has been developed using the most basic of elements in order to be sold at an affordable rate to people everywhere who have a variety of different needs. The Raspberry Pi can be used in the classroom to teach coding and computer programming, a very valuable skill set for students, some of whom will become future engineers and computer scientists. The price of the Raspberry Pi device is the best feature, as school boards can be easily convinced that it is a resource worth buying for every classroom.

It can also be used to create a variety of things that will improve your home, productivity and just be plain fun to create. The growing community of Raspberry Pi enthusiasts makes it easy for you to find fun things to do with this computer, and you may even be inspired to champion some experiments of your own. The Raspberry Pi Foundation has made tools and resources readily available to anyone who wants to be a part of this movement.

From computer technology experts to basic level beginners, people everywhere are raving about this amazing new development in the technological world. It is the future of technology in schools, and the future of making skills such as programming and coding common knowledge in every household. The Raspberry Pi can be a life changing experience for you, as long as you understand everything that you can do with it. If you are one of the people described above, or anyone else at all, this eBook is a valuable resource for you.

It is the one stop solution to all of the questions that you have about the Raspberry Pi, if you have heard of it and are not quite sure if you should make the commitment of purchasing one. It compiles all of the most valuable resources on and off line in one great information gold mine so that you do not have to spend hours of your time doing research before you can start enjoying the benefits of this great product.

Without a doubt, the Raspberry Pi is the next big thing in technological advancements, and you should be a part of it. Keep reading to learn the ins and outs of this unique creation, what you need to do once you have one, what you can do with one and how to get started with yours if you already have one. Be a part of the movement and stay on the cutting edge of technology with the Raspberry Pi, starting right now.

# Chapter 1: Some History of the Raspberry Pi

The Raspberry Pi was created in the United Kingdom by the Raspberry Pi Foundation. The foundation is a charity that was started in the year 2009, with the intention of championing the study of basic level computer science skills in schools. This was the main intention behind the creation of the Raspberry Pi.

The foundation was started when Eben Upton, Rob Mullins, Jack Land and Alan Mycroft among others, realized that the rate of students applying for universities with Computer Science as a major was declining, and that the students who did apply had a limited skill set. This problem was attributed to the lack of affordable and convenient computers in schools, so they realized that there was a necessity for a small computer that was also cost effective.

When they first began designing Raspberry Pi prototypes, they were extremely limited in their resources because processors for mobile devices at that time were quite expensive and had very little power. However, in 2008, the team began a partnership with Pete Lomas, MD and David Braben and, together, they founded the Raspberry Pi Foundation. Within three years, they were able to produce the Raspberry Pi Model B, and it sold more than two million units within two years.

The group expected students to learn programming using this affordable device, use the input/output function to control externally connected devices, and even be able to use it in robots or as a home media center. The Raspberry Pi was offered to schools at an introductory price of between US $ 20 and US $ 35, depending on the chosen model.

# A Brief Introduction to the Raspberry Pi

The Raspberry Pi is a single board computer about the size of a credit card. The original version is based on the Broadcom BCM2835 system on a chip. It originally came with 256 megabytes of RAM and some models have SD and MicroSD ports for extra storage capabilities. The Raspberry Pi comes in four different models: Model A, Model A+, Model B and Model B+.

Model A is the basic device and it has one USB port and 256 megabytes of RAM. Other ports it includes are a full size SD card port, HDMI output port and a composite video output port. It also has a 26 pin expansion header, a 3.5 millimeter audio jack, a camera interface port, an LCD display interface port and a microUSB power outlet for charging. Due to the absence of Ethernet output or other USB ports, the Raspberry Pi Model A uses less power than other models, specifically Model B or B+.

Raspberry Pi Model B was the higher end version of the Raspberry Pi up until July 2013, when Model B+ was released. It has everything that Model A has, except it has two USB ports and 512 megabytes of RAM, rather than 256. It also has one Ethernet port.

Model A+ was released in November 2014 and it is a slightly more advanced version of Model A. It comes with 40 General Purpose Input/Output (GPIO) pins. Just like Model A, it has only one USB port, no Ethernet output and 256 megabytes of RAM. It is, however, slightly smaller than the other models, at only 65 mm in length.

Model B+, a variation of Model B, was released in July 2014. It has four USB ports and 40 GPIO pins. It also has improved power circuits so that it can be attached to more powerful USB devices. The full size composite video connector is no longer needed, as this function has been replaced by a 3.5 millimeter combined audio and video jack. The full size SD card slot has been replaced with a MicroSD slot. Some other improvements over the Model B Raspberry Pi include current monitors which support hot-plugging, or adding components to the system without having to shut it down or interrupt system functions. It also has a current limiter on the 5V for HDMI, which means that VGA converters can also be used with the Raspberry Pi, back-powering will no longer be a problem, better audio DAC quality, and much more. Model B+ is the third revision of the Raspberry Pi and the last one using BCM2835.

## Educational Goals for the Raspberry Pi

This groundbreaking technology has been able to change information technology and computer science education in schools for the better. The invention of this device has come with many websites and resources in order to guide teachers through using it in primary schools to enhance computer science learning for students. With the Raspberry Pi, students are able to learn coding and explore other functionalities of computers in general. Some teachers believe that it helps students, especially girls, to see themselves as coders or computer scientists, many of whom do not imagine themselves in computer or engineering careers by the time they are leaving elementary school.

# Chapter 2: Raspberry Pi Capabilities

Each model of the Raspberry Pi comes with its own set of specifications and capabilities. In this chapter, we will look at each model and what it can do in detail.

## Model A

The earliest model of Raspberry Pi, model A was released onto the market with a price of US$25. The system-on-chip that it runs is the Broadcom BCM2835. In addition to that, this model comes with a central processing unit, graphics processing unit, digital signal processor, synchronous dynamic random-access memory and one USB port. Its central processing unit (CPU) is a 700 megahertz single core ARM1176JZF-S.

The graphics processing unit, or GPU, is Broadcom VideoCore IV at 250 megahertz, with OpenGL ES 2.0, MPEG-2 and VC-1. It also consists of 1080 pixels, H.264/MPEG-4 AVC high profile decoder and encoder. The model A Raspberry Pi features 256 megabytes of random access memory, which is shared with the graphics processing unit. There is only one USB port which is connected directly to the BCM2835 chip.

This model of the Raspberry Pi features a 15 pin MIPI (mobile industry processor interface) camera interface connector for video input, to be used with the Raspberry Pi camera or Raspberry Pi NoIR camera. For video outputs, it has HDMI ports, with fourteen different resolutions, from 640x350 to 1920x1200 pixels. It also has a variety of PAL (Phase Alternating Line) and NTSC (National Television System Committee) standards and composite video via an RCA jack. It also has two audio inputs and sends analog audio outputs through a 3.5 mm headphone jack and digital audio outputs through HDMI.

As far as storage, the Raspberry Pi Model A offers an SD, MMC and SDIO card slot, which gives you the option to save as much as you need. While there are no on board network connections for this model, the power ratings are 2.5 Watts, and it is powered using a microUSB port. For auxiliary devices, there is eight general purpose input and output elements and many others which can also be used for general purposes. These include a universal asynchronous receiver/transmitter and a serial peripheral interface bus with two chip selects.

This model measures 85.60 mm x 56.5 mm in size, not including connectors and weighs only 45 grams.

## Model A+

The Raspberry Pi Model A+ is slightly smaller than Model A, at 65 mm x 56.5 mm and 10 mm in height. It weighs 23 grams, and like model A, receives power using a micro USB port. It first entered onto the market at US$20 and uses the Broadcom BCM2835 operating system. Its CPU runs on a 700 megahertz single core ARM1176JZF-s, just like its immediate predecessor. It has 512 MB of memory, twice the built in storage space of model A, and has two USB ports. It shares its general processing unit specifications with the Raspberry Pi Model A, however.

Just like the Raspberry Pi Model A, it uses a 15 pin MIPI camera interface connector, and can be used with the Raspberry Pi camera or Raspberry Pi NoIR camera. As far as video outputs, Model A+ has all of the capabilities of Model A, with the addition of a 3.5 mm jack for composite video, which is shared with the analog audio output function. It has two audio input boards, and 2 for digital audio output, which use HDMI.

For added storage, the Raspberry Pi Model A+, offers a microSD slot, and while there is no on-board network, there are seventeen general purpose input/output pins along with HAT ID bus. For power ratings, this version of the Raspberry Pi has one Watt.

# Model B

The first version of the Raspberry Pi Model B features Broadcom BCM2835 as its operating system and a 700 megahertz ARM1176JZF-S CPU. Its general processing unit specifications do not differ at all from Models A and A+, but it comes with 512 megabytes of built in memory.

This version of the Raspberry Pi features two USB ports and like the model A, uses a SD/MMC/SDIO slot for added storage. It has a 10/100 megabit per second Ethernet USB adapter and eight general purpose input/output pins. It has a power rating of 3.5 Watts and also charges using a microUSB. It measures 85.60 mm x 56.5mm, excluding connectors and weighs 45 grams.

# Model B+

The Raspberry Pi Model B+ weighs the same 45 grams as the Model B, and is also 85.60 mm x 56.5 mm in size. It gets its power through a MicroUSB and has a power rating of three Watts. It features seventeen GPIO pins and HAT ID bus. In order to connect to the Internet, it uses a 10/100 megabit per second Ethernet USB adapter. There is an extra storage function available through a microSd slot, and it has two audio input boards and delivers audio output through a 3.5 mm phone jack or HDMI. It has the same video input capabilities as the other models and shares output functions with the latest version of Model B. It has four USB ports and offers 512 megabytes of on device memory. It uses the same specifications for the general processing unit, central processing unit, and systems as the Model A and A+, and it is sold for US$35.

# Chapter 3: Connecting and Booting up Your Raspberry Pi

Now that you know all of the capabilities of the various Raspberry Pi models, and you've got the nitty gritty technical stuff under your belt, it's time to understand how to use the Raspberry Pi.

## What You Need to Get Started

Before you get started, you will need a few things first. Some items that you will definitely need are and SD Card, a display cable, an Ethernet cable for Internet access, a keyboard and mouse and a power source.

The ideal SD Card will be a class 4 8 GB card. You may want to buy your SD card with the NOOBS (New Out of the Box System) installed, or you can download it from the Raspberry Pi website (http://www.raspberrypi.org). NOOBS is good, because it will get you started using your Raspberry Pi, quickly and easily. You cannot boot up your device without an operating system, and while you have other options which we will discuss in the next chapter, NOOBS is a perfect starter.

Any HDMI/DVI monitor will work as a display monitor for your Raspberry Pi. You can even use an old TV, as long as it still works. Your best option will be an HDMI cable, but you can also use an older connector for devices that use an earlier form of display input. A standard Ethernet cable will enable you to access the Internet using your Raspberry Pi. You can also use any kind of keyboard or mouse that connects with a USB to operate your system.

In terms of power, you should use a 5V microUSB as the power source for your Raspberry Pi. If you do not use a power supply with at least 5V, your Raspberry Pi will not perform at its best.

Some things that are not necessary, but will add to your Raspberry Pi experience are an Internet connection, which will allow you to update or download any software onto your Raspberry Pi with ease, and headphones or speakers which will work with the 3.5 audio output jack on the Raspberry Pi if you are not using an HDMI cable to connect to your display monitor.

# Setting Up Your Raspberry PI

Once you have everything you need, you will be ready to start using your Raspberry Pi. Setup is Easy, just follow a few simple steps.

**Step 1:** Insert your SD card into the appropriate slot on the Raspberry Pi.

**Step 2:** Plug in your USB keyboard and mouse.

**Step 3:** Turn on your monitor or TV and make sure that you have the right cables for video and audio input.

**Step 4:** Connect your display cable from your Raspberry Pi to the video monitor or TV.

**Step 5:** if your Raspberry Pi model is Ethernet capable, and you have Internet access, plug the Ethernet cable into the appropriate port.

**Step 6:** Plug your microUSB into your power source. Doing this will turn on your Raspberry Pi and allow it to start booting up.

**Step 7:** Once the system has booted up, you will be prompted to select an operating system. If you are using NOOBS, select this operating system and configuration. You can use a new guide available on the Raspberry Pi Foundation website in order to complete this task.

## How to Log in to Your Raspberry Pi

After you have successfully connected all of the parts of your Raspberry Pi and booted the system, you will be prompted to log in. The log in process is even easier than the setup process. There are only a few steps that you need to follow in order to log into your Raspberry Pi. The default log in for the Raspberry Pi is the user name 'pi' and the password is 'raspberry'. When you have been logged in, you will see a command line prompt which reads 'pi@raspberrypi~$'. Just type 'startx' and press *Enter*, and you will be ready to start using your Raspberry Pi.

# Chapter 4: Installing Your Operating System

There are many different operating systems that you can use with your Raspberry Pi. Ultimately, the one you choose will depend on what you would like to use your Raspberry Pi to do and some other factors, as well. Thankfully, your options are anything but limited. Here are a few of the most popular operating systems that can be used to run your Raspberry Pi device.

Raspbian is an operating system which can be downloaded for free from the Raspberry Pi Foundation website. It is a version of the highly popular Debian Linux operating system, created specifically to be used for the Raspberry Pi. There are many unofficial versions of this operating system that have been produced by users.

Another operating system that you use with your device is Arch Linux arm this is a version of Arch Linux which is built specifically for ARM processors. You can also use openELEC which is an acronym for open embedded Linux entertainment center. This is a linux-based operating system that runs XBMC digital media software.

Another choice that you have for operating your Raspberry Pi is Pidora. Other operating systems include RaspBMC, Minepeon, Kali Linux, open WRT for Raspberry Pi, Raspberry Digital Signage, and RISC OS Pi. each of these operating systems has its own advantages and disadvantages. We will discuss four of the most popular operating systems in detail, so that you can get and idea of which is the best for you and your intended use.

# Raspbian

This is without a doubt the most popular operating system in the Raspberry Pi user community. It is easy for even the most novice user to master and can be set up in no time. Also, because of its link to the Raspberry Pi Foundation, there are a lot more developers making software for it than any other operating system usable with the Raspberry Pi.

One of the most recognized benefits of this operating system, which places it ahead of its competitors, is that it has a wide range of teaching and learning tools. It comes with software like Scratch and Sonic Pi, which make it easy to learn the basics of coding, and it supports almost all supplemental hardware.

Another advantage of using this operating system is the fact that the majority of Raspberry Pi tutorials, projects and hardware are developed to be compatible with it. It is quite fast and not too bulky. In essence, this operating system has a ton of advantages compared to others and is very versatile.

# Pidora

When it was first released Pidora was known for being slow and sluggish and not able to keep up with the Raspberry Pi device uses. However, since its original debut, Pidora has been revised to remove bugs and has added a few elements that will allow it to run on Raspberry Pi software without a loss in functionality. The benefits of this operating system are that it is quite mature in terms of the fact that it has had time to work out all the kinks and is now stable and reliable.

Even though it cannot match the speed of Raspbian and Arch Linux, it is still one of the most popular operating systems for

Raspberry Pi. One big issue that this system has, is an extremely slow boot up from NOOBS It also does not have a lot of software compared to Raspbian. While more software is being developed everyday for Pidora users, it is still well behind some other operating systems in this respect. This operating system does come with all of the basics but it doesn't have enough accessories to make it a first choice if you will be using your Raspberry Pi for projects.

## RISC OS

This operating system is the reincarnation of the RISC, which was first developed by Acorn Computers to use on their ARM chip set. It was discontinued in 1998 and has been revived in the Raspberry Pi. While some users find it exciting to use this retro operating system, it does not have the capabilities all of the contemporary operating systems, such as Raspbian and Arch. Up until recently, it was difficult to perform simple functions, like taking screenshots, using this operating system.

It has been updated a few times and there has been an increase in available software, which has improved performance for this operating system. This operating system has a similar structure to Linux, using a three button system for opening menus which is yet another deviation from the standard operating systems today. This along with some other quirks can cause confusion for new users. Much like Pidora, this operating system is not well suited for projects.

## Arch Linux ARM

This operating system may seem a little bit intimidating. It has a steep learning curve, but it is perfect for users who want to learn the inner workings of Linux. There aren't many other operating systems that will give you the same opportunity. Arch has been on the market for about the same time as Raspbian. Unlike Raspbian, which gives users a wide selection of apps to choose from right away, this operating system will only come with a command line interface and a few basic extras. It allows the user to easily download only software that he or she may need, eliminating extra bulk and making it speedier than Raspbian. For this reason, arch is great for projects and applications.

It supports a large number of Raspberry Pi capabilities, including the Pi camera and the GPIO pins, which will allow you to use a plethora of accessories. Learning to navigate Arch will be a challenge for most new users, but don't let this scare you away. With some dedicated time to online tutorials, you should be able to master this operating system in no time.

# Chapter 5: Common Uses for Raspberry Pi

There are many different things that you can do with your Raspberry Pi. People get ideas for their Raspberry Pis from all over, whether it be from reading a book, watching or reading a tutorial, or seeing someone else complete a project. You may be convinced that the Raspberry Pi can be a useful device, but you may still be unsure as to what you can use it for. These common uses for the Pi may be a source of inspiration for you to begin working with and learning to use your Pi.

One thing that lots of people use their Raspberry Pi as, is a personal computer that they can use from the comfort of their living room. Once you connect your Raspberry Pi to a television monitor for display, you can use an operating system like OpenELEC and enjoy an at home mini movie theater like experience, using your tiny computer.

Another interesting thing you can use your Raspberry Pi for is retro gaming. If you are a gamer and you long to use the systems of yore, you might be interested in the RetroPie Project. This project will allow you to use your Raspberry Pi to imitate many old consoles including SNES and Mega Drive. While the set up can be taxing on earlier models of the Raspberry Pi and it does take some time, it will be worth it in the end. There are lots of classic games made available for free online that you can enjoy with your device.

An increasingly popular trend in Raspberry Pi use is robotics. The Raspberry Pi can be used to operate a robotic arm and maneuver other robots. There are several tutorials that can get you started on spearheading a robotics project of your own, something that you certainly will not regret.

The function that the Raspberry Pi is most well known for, and the one that it was created for, was its teaching programs. This is an extremely valuable tool for teaching and learning coding and programming. You can download programs like Scratch, which uses an easy to understand programming language. It is a great programming tool for children and novice adults to learn from, and it is perfect for creating complex programming projects.

# Chapter 6: Fantastic Raspberry Pi Projects

## NFC/RFID Reader

One thing that Pi users have found the Raspberry Pi handy for is working with Near Field Communication (NFC) cards as an attendance system. This is an invaluable use for small business owners, because buying attendance software can cost upwards of $700. For a company with ten to fifteen employees or less, this would not a good investment. However, by using the Raspberry Pi, which will not cost you more than $35, and less than ten other supplies, you will have a quick and easy way to keep track of your employee attendance records for a fraction of the cost. You can learn more about how to do this project yourself at http://m.instructables.com/id/Attendance-system-using-Raspberry-Pi-and-NFC-Tag-r/

## GPS Tracker

You can also use the Raspberry Pi as a tracker for your vehicle. Insurance and Security companies will track your car in case of theft at an added expense, but this project will allow you to use your Raspberry Pi for the same function for a smaller cost. The benefits of this project are almost self-explanatory, but it is indeed yet another amazing way to use this fantastic device. Find out how to do this by watching a video tutorial at https://logicethos.com/blog/raspberry-pi-run/

# Earthquake Detector

This is one project that can be truly described as lifesaving. Using the Raspberry Pi as an earthquake detector will ensure that you and your family are prepared for a natural disaster, especially if you live in an area that is prone to tremors. This Do It Yourself earthquake alarm was designed by one of the seismologists developing a large scale earthquake warning system for the state of California. You can make this project a reality for as little as $110. You can follow the simple, step-by-step directions for this innovative project on Professor Joshua Bloom's blog: http://5nf5.blogspot.com/2014/09/early-warning-device-of-earth quakes-and-other-maladies-for-everyone.html?m=1

# MP3 Player

Another great thing that you can do with your Raspberry Pi is turn it into an MP3 player. It is without a doubt a much cheaper alternative than MP3 players on the market today. Most people use their smart phones to listen to MP3 files, but if you do not own a smart phone, or yours is temporarily down, you can still enjoy listening to your favorite music, by learning this simple project for your Pi. You can find out how to turn your Raspberry Pi into an MP3 player using a flash drive at http://m.instructables.com/id/Implementation-of-MP3-player-usi ng-Raspberry-Pi/

# Desktop Computer

One of the most practical things that you can do with your Raspberry Pi is use it to replace a full-fledged desktop computer. Though slightly more complicated than just setting it up and throwing on an operating system, this is a cheap and easy way to replace a crashed or broken computer. You do not need many materials, and you can use and old keyboard and monitor. The Raspberry Pi itself is attached to the back of the monitor for a sleeker look than your average desktop. Find out how to do this at http://www.mdpub.com/pi/allinone/index.html

## Personal Web Server

Using your Raspberry Pi as a personal web server can have a wide range of advantages. You can use a personal web server to host a custom resume using HTML or PHP, or a personal landing page. You do not need any materials in order to do this, that are not included in the original list from  device set up chapter, which means it should be a breeze. Find out how to make this happen at http://www.instructables.com/id/Turning-your-Raspberry-Pi-into -a-personal-web-serv/

## Home Automation

You can use the Raspberry Pi device to set up a home automation system. In other words, you will be able to create a web app that will enable you to control the lights in your home remotely. This can be especially helpful during the holiday season when people might want to control their outdoor festive light display. The Pi uses the internet connection and the lights are turned on and off with a wireless remote. You can learn how to execute this project on http://m.instructables.com/id/Raspberry-Pi-GPIO-home-automat ion/

# Audiobook Player

If you love to listen to audiobooks, another great project that you can learn to do with your Raspberry Pi will turn it into an audiobook player. You can load your books one at a time, using a USB drive and listen to them easily. This will be especially useful to you if you do not like to use up the space in your other devices, such as smart phones, with audiobooks. You can learn how to build this here, at http://blogs.fsfe.org/clemens/2012/10/30/the-one-button-audiobook-player/

# Camera

If you have a passion for photography, you can also use your Raspberry Pi to add an embedded computer into your DSLR camera. You can use this project to do wireless tethering between you camera and another device. This will allow you to load images directly from your camera to your PC or tablet, as soon as you have shot them. You can also use it to control your camera from a distance using a smart phone from anywhere in the world. You can also set up your camera to take pictures within a specific time frame, during specific intervals of time. With this project, you can take automatic time lapse photos. Learn how to do this at http://www.davidhunt.ie/raspberry-pi-in-a-dslr-camera/

# Dog Treat Machine

For pet lovers, this project is a must! You can even use the Raspberry Pi to give your dog treats automatically, when you cannot do it yourself. This project functions by sending an email to a specific address. This project is slightly more complicated than others, using CAD design, fabrication, programming and more. If you are up to the challenge, you can find more information on this project at http://www.nyccnc.com/judd-treat-machine.html

## Raspberry Pi Lego Supercomputer

For this project, you will need a lot of skill, and a few more Raspberry Pis, but if you are up for it, it will be a lot of fun for the whole family. A researcher at the University of Southampton built a supercomputer, which was housed in a Lego racking system. The Lego racks were designed by the researcher and his six year old son.. The computer itself consists of 64 Raspberry Pis. The project has been made available to anyone interested on the university website. Just go to http://www.southampton.ac.uk/~sjc/raspberrypi/.

# Chapter 7: Common Programming Languages Used with Pi

In order to use the Raspberry Pi to the best of its capabilities, you will need to know some kind of programming, and if you do not know any, you will need to learn. There are a few common programming languages that are used with the Raspberry Pi, and in this chapter, you will learn a little bit about a few of them.

## Python

This is the programming language recommended by the Raspberry Pi foundation for beginners. It is one of the most popular programming languages that can be used with the Raspberry Pi. Python is a simple programming language and is very popular in academic settings. It is also noted as a productive code writing method. In addition to this it is versatile and uses less wording than other codes.

Some issues with Python, however, can be speed because it is an interpreted language. This slows down its execution speed, but it is quickly becoming optimized to run at the same speed as other programming languages. It is also not readily available for mobile platforms, so it may not be the best language to use for creating smart phone apps. And there are some design restrictions as well. Learn more about Python at https://www.python.org/

## Scratch

Scratch is the best programming language to get young children started with learning how to program. It consists of a drag and drop interface which allows you to build games, animation, and more without actually knowing programming. It is great for adults as well who would like to try their hand at programming, but do not have much prior knowledge about it. You can find lots of projects and tutorials at the Scratch website, http://scratch.mit.edu/ , which will give you and/or your students lots of great ideas for challenging your creativity, with this simple and easy to learn programming language.

## HTML5

HTML is the building block of the Internet, created by Tim Berners-Lee as a means for scientists to share documents with one another. It controls the way a web browser displays pages, and allows you to form links between them. HTML5 is the latest version of this programming language, and if you are able to learn it, you can do things with your Raspberry Pi like embed videos and audio into web pages and write apps that will run on smart phones or tablets with ease. The Raspberry Pi Foundation has developed a web browser specifically designed to support HTML5. With this programming language, you can use the Raspberry Pi to create tabs, do two-dimensional rendering, and accelerated image and video decoding. Learn more about HTML5 at http://www.w3schools.com/html/html5_intro.asp

# Chapter 8: Creating Games with the Raspberry Pi

One of the most exciting things that can be done with the Raspberry Pi is using it to create and play games. You can do everything from recreating classic games to designing your own custom games. You can also run emulators in order to turn your Raspberry Pi into one of your favorite retro gaming centers.

You can easily recreate several classic games on your Raspberry Pi and enjoy your favorite arcade classics to relive your older gaming days, or even try out games that you have heard a lot about but have never gotten to play for yourself. In short, the Raspberry Pi can easily become the gamer's dream device, with the right information.

If you are not ready to create your own games for the Raspberry Pi, there is a wide range of games available for you to install from the Raspberry Pi store. Many programming languages also offer easy to learn add-ons that will specifically guide you in creating games for the Raspberry PI. One such add on is Pygame, which is made available by Python. As mentioned earlier, Python is the primary programming language for educational use of the Raspberry Pi.

Pygame assists users in developing games using Python programming. For instance, it improves the ease of image handling with its Sprite class, as well as controlling audio within a game and creating your game to work with added hardware such as a joystick or controller. Some more complex games maybe a little challenging to create, but you can easily put together something resembling Angry Birds, or another simple game that you enjoy on other platforms.

You can use an emulator to play hundreds of games on your Raspberry Pi. You can create one that will allow you to play games from the 1980s and 1990s such as those developed for early Apple computers, Atari, Game Boy Advance, Intellivision, Playstation 1 and SuperNES. If you are a fan of handheld game consoles, you can even build one that is powered by your Raspberry Pi. Gaming consoles like the Game Boy Pocket, which is no longer being manufactured but still a fan favorite can be recreated using the Raspberry PI and a few other elements. You can make either a color version or the classic black and white.

If you are a parent or an educator, you will be interested in using the Raspberry Pi to create a dedicated Minecraft Machine. Minecraft is a very popular game in which you can build your own world, and children love it. It has simple graphics, that make it a breeze to run on Raspberry Pi, and some of the latest versions of the Raspbian operating system come with a version of this game pre-installed, and optimized to run on the Pi.

## Game Tutorials and Instructables

In this section, you will find a lot of helpful links to get you started with turning your Raspberry PI into a virtual game machine.

### Handheld Raspberry Pi Game Console

This project will turn you Pi into one of your favorite old school game consoles. This is basically a Raspberry Pi operated Game Boy Pocket. Find a tutorial for this project at http://lifehacker.com/how-to-build-a-handheld-raspberry-pi-pow ered-game-cons-1663675758

Make Your Own Game on Raspberry Pi

For the more creative and adventurous Pi users, this tutorial will help you to us Python coding to create a custom game for Raspberry PI. You will learn how to use the Pygame add-on in order to do so, at http://www.linuxuser.co.uk/tutorials/make-a-game-on-raspberry-pi

## Turn Your Raspberry PI into an Emulator

If you want to explore or revisit the world of vintage video games, this project is perfect for you. It will show you how to turn your Pi into the optimal retro gaming machine. You will be able to run games for Game Boy Advance, Atari and SNES using RetroPie. Find a tutorial for this project on http://makezine.com/2015/01/08/atari-emulator-uses-raspberry-pi-to-play-800-games-and-more/

## Dedicated Minecraft Machine

You can use your Raspberry Pi as an around the clock server for your Minecraft game. This is a great way to enjoy your Minecraft experience to the max. You can let friends and family build in your would by leaving your server on 24/7 and increase control over your multiplayer game much better than you can using a public server. Learn how to do this at http://www.howtogeek.com/173044/how-to-run-low-cost-minecraft-on-a-raspberry-pi-for-block-building-on-the-cheap/

# Chapter 9: Getting Creative with your Pi

Once you have a basic level knowledge of how to work your way around your Raspberry Pi, and a little bit more of programming and application development, you can turn your Raspberry Pi into a manifestation of your wildest ideas. This device is teeming with opportunities for invention and creativity. All you need is a bit of inspiration. To start you off, here are a few of the creative things that people around the world have come up with to do with their own Raspberry Pis.

## Creating a Custom Case

The Raspberry Pi does not come with a case, and it is important for you to get one so that your Pi stays safe. You can buy a case, or you can build a custom case for your Raspberry Pi. You can use a Punnet case, which you can find a printable design for online. This case is easy to make using thick paper or card stock, and it will not cost you a lot to make. Pi users are also making cases out of Legos.

Of course, you can always buy a case online or upcycle any old hardware you have around the house. Handheld game consoles like the Nintendo Game Boy and old routers can all make exceptional cases for the Raspberry Pi. You can even use old toys and music players with a little bit of tweaking. You can purchase a hobby case with the right dimensions to fit your Raspberry Pi from quite a few outlets. You can also find a Lego kit to build a custom case for your Pi. Here are some links that will be helpful in making the choice for your Raspberry Pi case:

www.piholder.com

www.pibow.com

www.thedailybrick.co.uk/lego-sets/custom/lego-custom-raspberry
-pi-case.html

# Make Your Own Smart Phone

Did you know that you can use your Raspberry Pi as the base of a smart phone? Raspberry Pi user, David Hunt, championed this project. He uses an Adafruit touchscreen and a Sim900 GSM/GPRS module to make phone calls. If this relatively cheap project appeals to you, check it out at his website. It may not be the most simple project, but it will definitely be a lot of fun to build.

http://www.davidhunt.ie/piphone-a-raspberry-pi-based-smartpho
ne/

# Otto: A Raspberry Pi Powered Digital Camera

You can also use your Pi to take animated still photos. Otto is a customizable digital camera that is powered by the Raspberry Pi. It features many of the functions that your phone camera probably does. It takes animated GIFs, stills and videos. You will be able to automatically sync your photos over WiFi for easy sharing with you friends and family. Otto's modes have a lot of settings that give you the power to control literally everything about your photographing experience. See more information on Otto here: http://nextthing.co/otto.html

# Audio Twitter Feed

If you are a big twitter user, you will love this idea. Magpi Radio uses text-to speech to read tweets as they come in on various channels. You can change the channels by clicking the beak, and you can even favorite tweets and respond to them. This is yet another groundbreaking device that is powered by the Raspberry Pi. See how the Pi inspired the invention of Magpi Radio on http://itp.nyu.edu/~wdl225/work/?p=275

# Chapter 10: Top Success Tips When Working with a Pi

In order to get the full range of advantages from your Raspberry Pi, you will want to know what to do and what not to do. This will ensure ease of use and you will be able to enjoy your Pi to the fullest. Here are a few things that you can do to make sure that your Raspberry Pi experience is a success.

## Tip #1: Handle Your Raspberry Pi with Care

No matter what plans you have for your Raspberry Pi, remember to take very good care of it. It is quite small, but this does not mean that it cannot be as easily damaged as any other computer. It is vulnerable to damage from static electricity, as well as dropping and scratching.

In order to avoid doing any damage to your valuable Pi, be sure to remove jewelry and garments that may attract static before handling it. You should also try to handle your device in an area that is clean and free of dust, and of course, with clean hands. Once you have properly encased your Pi, it shouldn't be much more trouble to take care of than any other device.

## Tip#2: Safely Shut Down and Boot Your Pi

Another thing that Raspberry Pis have in common with other computers is being prone to the dangers of being shut down and started up improperly. Because the Raspberry Pi's main storage unit is an SD card, turning it off by unplugging the power supply will almost definitely corrupt its operating system. If this happens, you will have to reinstall it.

This can easily be avoided by using the shut down menu option, or entering the 'sudo shutdown -h now' in the command line. Once the computer has been properly shut down, you can remove the power cable. You can safely boot up your Pi by making sure that the SD card is properly inserted before turning it on.

# Tip# 3: Check Your Power Supply

Another tip for using the Raspberry Pi successfully, is making sure that you have an adequate power supply. The Raspberry Pi uses a microUSB for power, which was selected by the foundation due to its universal use. All android phones charge using a microUSB, as well as kindle devices. It is also the standard charging port in Europe. However, there are certain specifications that are needed for the cable that you will be using to charge your Pi. It should have an output of at least 5V and 700 mA.

If you are not sure, double check with your local electronics store, as not every microUSB cable is the same. Using an inadequate power supply will cause your Pi to have running issues, from start up errors to problems with the keyboard or Ethernet function. To avoid these problems, resist the urge to use whatever microUSB cable you have laying around the house without first checking to make sure that it meets the specific requirements outlined for your Pi.

# Chapter 11: Raspberry Pi Events, Communities and Meet Ups

One of the greatest things about the age of technology is the ability to become a part of a global community in order to share your passion for something, or learn new things. This is possible for Raspberry Pi users, especially, and it will certainly enhance your Raspberry Pi experience to keep abreast of Pi related events, forums and meet ups. Here are a few Pi community links that will likely be of interest.

## Raspberry Jam

Raspberry Jams are organized by Raspberry Pi users in order to share knowledge about the Pi and meet other Pi enthusiasts. Attending a Raspberry Jam is an engaging way to learn more about the Raspberry Pi and what you can do with it. You will also be able to meet others who are as passionate about this device as you are. You can find a map with Raspberry Jam locations, to find out if there will be any in your area. There is also a calendar that lists upcoming events. You can find these resources at http://www.raspberrypi.org/jam/ If there are no upcoming events near you, you can run your own Jam, as anyone is allowed to.

All you have to do is find a place ,set a date and time and you will be able to attract Raspberry Pi enthusiasts in your area. There is a detailed list of guidelines for running your own Jam at http://www.raspberrpi.org/jam/how/ . It addresses frequently asked questions about things such as venue and sponsoring, as well as organizing talks and ticket prices. You can also read about featured Jams if you are contemplating attending one and would like to see what it will be like and add your Jam to the website database, once it has been organized.

## Raspberry Pi Forums

If you have questions about your Pi, or would like to learn about the challenges some other members of the Pi community have faced, in order to arm yourself with knowledge, you can check out one of the several Raspberry Pi forums online. The Raspberry Pi Foundation website hosts several, covering topics such as troubleshooting, beginners tips and interesting projects. Members of the Pi community share their ideas and insights for your benefit, and once you have mastered your Pi, you may feel comfortable doing the same.

You can also engage in forums hosted on other sites, such as XDA forums. They have a discussion dedicated to Raspberry Pi hacking and development. You can also check out eLinux.org which has a wiki page about the Pi, and OpenELEC media center for information about several Raspberry Pi based discussions. Here are some links to a few websites to get you started as a member of the Raspberry Pi online community:

http://www.raspberrypi.org/forums/

http://elinux.org/RPi_Hub

http://openelec.tv/forum/124-raspberry-pi

http://forum.xda-developers.com/hardware-hacking/raspberry-pi

# Raspberry Pi Meetups

To learn about other Raspberry Pi Meetups, you can go to meetup.com and check out some of the many Raspberry Pi related meetup groups. If you weren't able to find anything in your area on the Raspberry Pi Foundation Website, this site is your best bet. There are 242 groups in 172 cities all over the world that will be meeting up to discuss the Raspberry Pi, among other topics, according to the website. To see for yourself, go to http://raspberry-pi.meetup.com/

# Chapter 12: Fantastic Online Resources for the Raspberry Pi

As evidenced by the many links presented to you thus far, there is quite a wealth of information about the Raspberry Pi to be found online. This chapter will give you a few extra resources to get you started and beyond, with your Raspberry Pi device.

## Web Resources and Blogs

For educational use of the Raspberry Pi, one of the best places to find resources is the Raspberry Pi Foundation website. They feature links to resources for teaching and learning using the Raspberry Pi, as well as classroom friendly projects. Go to http://www.raspberypi.org/resources/

The MagPi is a downloadable free magazine, dedicated to being a resource for Raspberry Pi fans. You can download the latest issue at http://www.raspberrypi.org/magpi/ and you can also purchase it in print form if you would prefer to own a hard copy.

Reddit, home of one of the most extensive online communities, is a great place to find news about the Raspberry Pi, as well as great project ideas. You will find links to YouTube videos and instructables, and if you get stuck you will certainly be able to find someone with answers. www.reddit.com/r/raspberry_pi

On MakeUseOf, you can find articles on a wide range of topics related to the PI. You will be able to learn about making retro gaming centers, cloud storage devices, and much much more using your Raspberry Pi. You will also be able to find tutorials about how to make attractive custom cases to house your Pi. There is even a step by step guide to getting started with the Raspberry PI.

http://www.makeuseof.com/tag/raspberry-pi-creditcard-sized-arm-computer-25/

You should also take a look at blogs about the Raspberry Pi, of which there are many to choose from. One notable blog is on Adafruit.com. Here you can find all of the latest updates about the Raspberry Pi, as well as a few interesting projects for your databases. https://blog.adafruit.com/category/raspberry-pi/

Lifehacker, a notable blog site on a variety of topics, has a dedicated Raspberry Pi section, which will certainly be of interest to you. This is also a great place to check for emerging projects being done with the Pi, that you might like to try yourself. http://lifehacker.com/tag/raspberry-pi

*Raspberry Pi Kid* is a blog run by a thirteen year old. The epitome of the Raspberry Pi Foundation's aims, this kid talks about everything having to do with the Pi, from new developments, to failed experiments. Find this blog at https://raspberrypikid.wordpress.com/

## Print Resources

If you are interested in offline resources, there are some very useful books and magazines available about the Raspberry Pi.

*Raspberry Pi User Guide* by Eben Upton and Gareth Halfacre is co-written by one of the co-creators of the Raspberry PI, so you can imagine all of the great and valid information there is to be found in this book.

*Haynes Raspberry Pi Manual* takes a look at hardware, software, and projects that can be done using the Raspberry Pi. It is authored by Dr. Gray Girling, a Broadcom engineer who was closely involved in the Pi's development.

You might also want to take a look at *Programming the Raspberry Pi: Getting Started with Python*, a book that will five you all of the tools you need to learn Python and become a Raspberry PI programing master. This book will teach you how to use the Pi's GPIO port to interface with external devices and complete exciting projects, like building an LED clock.

# Conclusion

Thanks for downloading this book.

Hopefully, it was able to give you a comprehensive set of information about the Raspberry Pi, its capabilities, and everything that you can do with it. It should inspire you to jump into the world of Raspberry Pi.

Once again, the Pi is an amazing tool that can be used in a variety of ways, from simple media streaming to preparing for natural disasters, and in a variety of settings, including schools and homes. You can use it to express your creativity and pique your imagination. It can be used to create games and play games. Frankly, the amount of fantastic projects that you can complete with your Pi are almost endless.

Using a Raspberry Pi will help you to learn to use many different computer programming languages, and you have many operating systems to choose from as well, depending on what you would like to accomplish. Use the resources provided to learn even more, and inspire those around you as well as other Pi enthusiasts or beginners, with stories of your journey, its challenges, and of course, your triumphs.

With this book, and the Raspberry Pi, almost anything is possible!

www.ingramcontent.com/pod-product-compliance
Lightning Source LLC
Chambersburg PA
CBHW060932050326
40689CB00013B/3064